The Silence
Before the Whisper Comes

The Silence
Before the Whisper Comes

Bruce Kauffman

First Edition

Hidden Brook Press
www.HiddenBrookPress.com
writers@HiddenBrookPress.com

Copyright © 2013 Hidden Brook Press
Copyright © 2013 Bruce Kauffman

All rights for poems revert to the author. All rights for book, layout and design remain with Hidden Brook Press. No part of this book may be reproduced except by a reviewer who may quote brief passages in a review. The use of any part of this publication reproduced, transmitted in any form or by any means, electronic, mechanical, photocopied, recorded or otherwise stored in a retrieval system without prior written consent of the publisher is an infringement of the copyright law.

The Silence Before the Whisper Comes
by Bruce Kauffman

Editor – Carolyn Smart
Cover Photograph – Eleanor Leonne Bennett
Cover Design – Richard M. Grove
Layout and Design – Richard M. Grove

Typeset in Garamond

Printed and bound in Canada

Library and Archives Canada Cataloguing in Publication

Kauffman, Bruce, author
    The silence before the whisper comes / Bruce Kauffman.

Poems.
ISBN 978-1-897475-98-0 (pbk.)

    I. Title.

PS8621.A685S55 2013   C811'.6   C2013-901681-3

A Meadow

It was a riverside meadow, lush, from before the hay harvest,
On an immaculate day in the sun of June.
I searched for it, found it, recognized it.
Grasses and flowers grew there familiar in my childhood.
With half-closed eyelids I absorbed luminescence.
And the scent garnered me, all knowing ceased.
Suddenly I felt I was disappearing and weeping with joy.

Czeslaw Milosz
from *Finding a River*
Ecco Press, 1995

Contents:

preface – *p. xi*

– caught between – *p. 1*
– pathway – *p. 2*
– wet – *p. 5*
– blue – *p. 6*
– raven – *p. 10*
– mesa verde – *p. 11*
– braided – *p. 14*
– book – *p. 16*
– in French – *p. 17*
– transition – *p. 19*
– song – *p. 21*
– life – *p. 22*
– sound – *p. 23*
– all – *p. 27*
– blue rain – *p. 28*
– humility – *p. 29*
– doa – *p. 30*
– day 1643 – *p. 33*
– answered – *p. 37*
– late last night – *p. 38*
– windsong – *p. 40*
– droplet – *p. 42*
– other lives – *p. 43*
– crossroad – *p. 48*
– elders – *p. 50*
– wing – *p. 51*
– time passage – *p. 53*
– red wind – *p. 55*
– creation – *p. 56*

– evening – *p. 57*
– forest – *p. 58*
– down – *p. 61*
– echo – *p. 62*
– again – *p. 63*
– name – *p. 66*
– northern lights – *p. 68*
– in passing – *p. 72*
– shadows – *p. 74*
– behind – *p. 77*
– remembering – *p. 78*
– lucid blue – *p. 80*
– other side – *p. 81*
– forests – *p. 83*
– other – *p. 84*
– whispers – *p. 85*
– renaissance – *p. 88*
– distance – *p. 92*

Author Bio – *p. 96*
Front Cover Photographer Bio – *p. 99*

preface

I cannot say for sure if it's a human condition to search for, to seek softness. Perhaps it's only in those times of "hardness" that we seek it, find solace in it. Perhaps it's always there, somewhere inside—just waiting to be recognized, remembered. And as I say this, I realize it's foolish for me to assume, to place my own personal passion for its touch, its presence on all other beings.

But it is from this that the poetry in this book comes. The passive softness and the realized fullness of both whisper and silence, and in it the voices then coming and spilling themselves out as ink on the page.

I am here, as in nearly all of my poetry, simply the translator, the inscriber, the conduit, the pen.

The voices, then—perhaps the muse, the muses, or simply that coming from and through prolonged, profound periods within that silence—a search below the artificial and superficial, into that inner core of essence—and in an effort of trying not simply to paint or to define, to un-define instead.

In this, all, for me to take credit for these poems is very much like the horizon claiming credit for the sunrise.

But it is, with the voices and words coming at me through the rain in the distance, here that the flow of the pen moves. It is in that silence, that fullness of it, that I understand in its breadth and its depth, that full and true silence is no longer the opposite of either sound or even noise, but instead of emptiness.

And perhaps, whisper, then—our attempt at intimately reaching back in voice to it.

caught between

between the walls
holding everything
      out
holding all things
      in

you sit in
the emptiness
today calling
      itself "home"

and you cannot
decide
if the wind blowing full
through your window
      open

is showing you
      how to leave

or telling you
      why to stay

pathway

is it
      fear or
      comfort or
      disinterest or
      discontent

that keeps
      paths empty
      or walked only
            part way

is it destiny
      that keeps paths
      from crossing

            or eyes
            not watching or

eyes
not looking
      far enough
      to see or

eyes
over ever-
present crossings
      looking beyond
      too far ahead......

i
not the creator
of this life
      instead the follower
      observer
            passive

i
more the butterfly
than the iron horse

i
        of the caterpillar
eye
        of the cocoon
        watched the full
                moon
        the arid starry
                sky
        envisioned desert
                forest
                river
                rock

and my heart
wanting to witness
wanting to see
wanting to touch
        dreamed of wings

                dreamed of the echo
                of other wings
                        calling back

dreamed

dreamed

until one morning
>   as sand melted
>   to water
i awoke atop
the dew laden limb
>   of the lilac bush

looking back under
a not so distant ledge
>   at my open
>   cracked
>   and empty bed and

knowing i
>   would not live
>   forever —

but
>   for the first
time
ever
>   wanting to

wet

watching
        here
on this edge
        of all edges

the day
still uncertain
        of which way
        it will fall

my words
        here
becoming
        like water, clear

then silent

but in the night
from within
coming again
becoming

this new language
and its only sound
that of
some distant and
echoed waterfall

blue

on a day
when blue
  was falling
from the sky
  dissolving itself
  melting away
    from, into

losing itself
drowning all colour

everything
then turning
  itself simply into
  pale and charcoal
    hues of grey

i was young

i watched

and those of us
who remembered
  colour after
  talked about it
but in words
  hollow
words without meaning
words without depth
  falling off walls
  and air, echoless

and when those
of the new ears
        when those borne
        of the grey light
listened
to their elders who
in remembrance then
        spoke of colour
those words
        had only the sound
                of slight breath
        a pause
                in a sentence

and then
to the new ears
the sentence
        made no sense

        with judgement then
        about everything said

but i tell you
        reader
that those things
without ears
        do not judge
        but remember
the rock
the river
the soil
the trees

the trees

the trees remember
        colour
they remember who
        they were

        who they are

they remember how
        their ancestors grew
        taller to see above
to see all
        to get closer
to the blue
        in the sky

and i tell
you about
        how in
        whispered breath
i remember
        colour
        true colour

i can see it
as it was
        with my eyes
        closed
and now
        even with them
        open as well

and you, reader,
        argue
that you too
        look out your window
        and see your world
        in colour

and i weep
as i again
    explain
that you are seeing
    but lines of grey

reader, you see
    i am two hundred
    years already
    in the grave and
last night
while you slept
    dreaming about
    your colours

these words were
    arriving at you

delivered
    on the backs
    of the drops
        of indigo rain

behind thunder
in the distance
    you never heard

and in those burgundy
hours of the night
    that you can
    no longer see

raven

the spirit of the raven
still silently flies overhead
carrying with it pictures
      of daylight
      and poe

pictures

pictures of which
i have seen only
      an edge

and while looking
straight into the raven
      spirit's eyes
i gently run my finger
across both pictures' edge and

i then realize
that poe
      could not wait
but I am left

still believing
that daylight will wait
      forever

mesa verde

here
        on the mesas
in the truth
        of cliff
        of home

here
in the northern breath
        of the incas
        the aztec
        the mayan

in the fainter breath
        of the iroquois
        the huron
              the mohican

in the shallow breeze
in the truth
of the only breath
        of the anasazi
              here

under the blue sky
and the four moons

we knew
        what the earth
        could give and
in any single day
we offered thanks
        to the spirits
        of the clouds

and we knew
        what the earth
        could take
and from her
we took only time
and offered our thanks
        to season
        to moon

and we awoke
eyes open each day
        in that space
        of all time
but, we, blind still
on this backside
        of distance

behind that edge
        coming
and carrying the ultimate
        whisper of death

we did not know
that when our words
left our lips
        that they would not
        forever be tied
        to earth
        to sky

we did not know
until too late about
        the extinction of language
        the dust of tradition
until
the rain forgot itself

until
we lost the green
        in ourselves

until
the ground fell barren
        the grass thinner
        thinner
thinned
to but pathways
        of peyote
        and sage and

you
now stand
        here today
beside
a similar footprint
        familiar
        the same

footprint imprinted
engraved
        in rock
a wet teardrop
        beside and

you know

you know and

you then
left wondering
exactly when
and how
in that time
you'd been here
        before

braided

in the summer heat
she again decides
to braid her hair
straight
down
the back of her neck

and this time
as she glides and weaves
her hands instinctively
she for an instant
remembers
        as a child, her mother braiding
        her hair for her and for the first time
        and there then with her own
        clumsy fingers trying to imitate behind

today
she finishes
moves into the next room
to her husband waiting

and as they together go out the door
she instinctively reaches
        for his lifeless
            uncaring hand and

she looks up into the mirrored
edge of sky and sees the moon's
reflection on the other side

and she
for this first time in her life
understanding fully both
        braid
        and hand
and wishing she could go back

and start all the braids
in her life
        all over again

book

as our pages
   turn
  slip

and we
among them
   ever-present

yesterday becoming
   no longer
    the noun that it was

but instead
   verb in its passing

and but adjective
   in its pieces left

in french

even in another language
i do not know

i could
        read your mind

for an instant visit
every dream you'd ever had
in places i had never been
all vivid
        lucid

and you sat across the room
in conversation
i could not understand

but i could
read in your lips
        not moving
between your smiles
        vacant
an unsettledness

and as your fingers
slid unconsciously
        across your lips

        across your cheeks

        and through your hair

i could see
in your fingers

your mouth

your eyes

all of you within
and all of that within unmet

an emptiness

a yearning

and for just an instant
as you rose to leave

i caught your eye

and there
acknowledgement

and in confession
        mutual

mine
that i'd seen

that i knew

yours
that you knew
that i'd seen

that you knew
that i knew

transition

chapters

now camping
in this house
that never sleeps

quiet only
for an hour at 5am

in that quiet hour
i sit on my bed
        this couch
a small kitten
waiting
        at my feet

as i place my journal
on my knees
begin to write
the kitten snuggles
on my lap between
sniffing and then
watching the pen
        her eyes then focused
        on letters, words slowly
        scrolling across the page

        transfixed

        seeing poetry
        for her first time.....

and for an instant
i remember myself
as a very small child
looking up at the sky and

for the first time seeing
        the colour blue

song

i, passive observer
        cautious

wanting, but
        not knowing
        how

never the conqueror
but neither the victim

yet the wind
at my back

still sings through my open
window at night

songs
of what and
how much
        i have missed

life

this life
this path
  both chosen
  pulled into

somehow circular
but always
at each point
upon four corners

  destiny
  karma
  illusion
  free will

memories fly
above us
cascading spirals
and then into flat lines

as we retrieve in fragments
  at points
shared time between
these overlapping
spheres of
  bone and faith

this

this

this transparent present

this forever past

this occasional future

sound

i.

these tunnels
      coming
drawing me
      in

these not
those with
light at the end
      another side
      a passing through

no, these
the kind
with a deepening
      darkness

      damp stagnant
      mildew air

these the kind
that words
      make

these the kind
the silence
      keeps

ii.

my eyes
accustomed now
        to this wetness
        this hollow light
this seeing
objects
in the dark
        before
        they appear
seeing others
still
that do not
        come

my hearing
        magnified
        intensified

hearing
        acute
this
        different sound

this

not the sobbing
        child in afghanistan
but the sound
the tears make
as they roll
        down her cheek

this

not the thunder
beneath the elephant's
.....hooves but
in her last walk
the sound of the sand
crunching
stretching
sifting into
.....the spaces
brushing against
.....the coarse white
.....hair on her feet

this

not the sound
the wind makes
in gales
.....as it crosses
.....the lake
but the sound
the opening
the space
.....makes before
.....the wind comes into

this

not the calling
the screeching
the cawing
  of bird
but the sound
of its down
  rustling against
  the straw in its nest
that sound of
its first new skin
pushing outward
  against the cracked
  edge of egg

and this

i sitting here
now
hearing no longer
  the words

  or the silence

but the breath
in those spaces
  between

all

    that which has
        always been
    coming into this
        moment waiting
    seeping
        through hollow cracks
        in an open sky and

    yes, today,

    all that there is
        whispers

blue rain

with this page before me
waiting to catch moisture
there are times when words
no longer freely fall
        from an
            ordinary sky

and on those days i take
the lavender bowl to
the barrel beneath
the corner eve of the house

i draw from barrel's surface
the wet words
floating there

then with tongs
dripping black ink
i separate and pull words
        from the bowl
and place them gently
        on a page

they
content
to be there

but their heart
        is still floating
        in yesterday's sky

humility

there is a beauty
that forgets itself
displaces surface
remembers texture

watches
other beauty

a beauty relaxed
as it lies
in this field
of humility

as a beauty
silent
without mirror
       and unaware

doa

now
four days since
it happened and

for the past three days
i have walked
by this spot on this road
where you had crossed
into the path
of that which was
        already coming
of that which
        you were unaware
of that which was
        so much larger than you

and you
in an instant
became invisible
        to the naked eye

and i but three weeks
        before
walked here
        along this spot
feeling then
a fullness inside
        intense

the blue sky there
then
        funnelling up
behind this circle of trees
        of different names
        different shapes
in an ever widening
vortex
        of colour and

i still then
only believing
        in sky
        and tree
did not see
the colour of
the painted lips
of a tunnel
waiting to inhale
        a life away

and

i stand now
beyond the held breath
of these swollen
closed lips

i stand now
touching both sides
of the wind
      of beauty blowing

beside these
remnants
of your last seconds here

the flowers laid
      beside the curb
      at the spot where
      you had crossed

the tracks, the marks
      left on the street

the wafting vapour of
      silence and loss
      in the air above

and i
seeing now
through newer
tear-filled eyes
only that which
      can be seen
      with a naked heart

day 1643

imprisoned

isolation

the darkness
   stretches

    still reaching
    to find
      its own depth

i count the days
   here
by the glint
   of light lasting
   a few moments
     through a small
     crack in an
       outside wall

i assume
   it is the
   sun rising

    but again
    i assume

it could be
   the guards
   who know
     already
      about the cracks
      in the wall

    perhaps
        they are shining
        their own lights
           through their own
           darkness

      to amuse
        or
      to confuse
        or

        worse

i am still
now trying
    to learn
    the language
        of the insects

        they no longer
           speak with me
        but i believe
           they know
           that i listen

i have scratched
    the beginnings
    of their alphabet
        their languages
with a scattered
    nail found

etching them along
    the sides
    of the wall

      now

for some unborn
child

   i guess

   for they tell me
   i can never leave

etching languages
for some future
heart
   with eyes
   and legs
      attached

   and

      the same paths
      wandered

the insects know
already though

who this new
person
   is
   will be

they have spoken
   of him
they are anxious

they wait

and they speak
   of how

   they will build
   their new nests
     from my dust
     and my bones
     and

place them

within the crack
   of the outside
   wall

answered

coming to this place

the same place
i always come
early
at dawn
on sunday mornings

passively open
expecting
       nothing

until the rising sun
pulls my attention
from the street that was
as i look up into a pale blue sky and

from its centre
the calling
of an almost invisible
       crescent moon and
in its wave of languages
raining down and washing
through
come the whispers
of all other eyes
watching

and come the answers
       to all questions lost

late last night

the full moon
blood red

then orange
vanilla
rising over
reflecting itself
        its colour atop
the eastern shore
        of lake ontario

then white
        on black

a lone grey owl

silhouette flying
against the evening
        across the line
        of newly risen
moon

and here

casting its shadow
through my window

opening a space
in the air
letting voice
        slip through

        whispers

        the maker of dreams

        and filling
        a space in the darkness
        with what comes

windsong

in the echoes
of the breeze
ever gently
      swirling lives
from east to west
and west to east
tracing autumn leaves

morning turns
to afternoon

beside an empty fireplace
beneath a glass covered sky

time lost between
words lost
between themselves
      between the spaces
      between

and just outside
      these windowed walls
      these soft chairs
      these soft words
          this soft air

a shared glance past
the glass of the day
      the light snow falling
      gently
      at angles and

the earth reminds
        of herself
        on the outside
as time sings that it
both is and is not
illusion
        and

with the wind
now
at our backs

droplet

    we do not see
    fail often to remember
    the faint shadow
    of colour and light
    constantly, eternally
        flowing
    trails of ourselves
        gently falling, remaining
        with a scent of our own
        upon all the places been
        all people seen, unseen and
            each of them wearing
            their own trails, scents
            as we follow

    i, here now,
    in the middle
        of all things
    wrapped in the whisper
        of rainbows
    under this dense
    grey fog sky
    beneath leafless maple
        and on the tip
        of a dew-laden twig
    i, this droplet of water,
        hang suspended

        waiting for the sky
        to pull me up into and

        with the full
        of the earth
        calling below

other lives

i.

before the
burgundy sun
these blue voices
in the wind

those grey other
voices rising
up out of the earth

each
then mixing
        in an autumn air

voices meld

their threads dancing
        gently in that other
        broader air around

this new texture

these separate threads
each wrapping around and

each thread
a different texture
a different shade
        of every colour

each having
        its own gentle vibration
flowing outward
        from the point
        of the word it was and

all of these threads
arrive
        come to me
wrap around
        then blow
        straight through

ii.

before the dawn
while you sleep
      your voice
      your words
are arriving in
      their original
      form

before your lips
have even given them sound

before you believe
      you own them

in your sleep
your heart
had already
given them up
to the air

to wear
      to feel

and as you
awaken
lost in the
lips of your mind
your answers
in that embryo
      that voice of silence
are alive outside
      adrift in the breeze

iii.

and in the morning
      you come
you who still are
      blind to the air
      unaware of its texture

you
who attempt
to tell me
      about water

you
who has never
      touched a drop
      from the river
who
has never seen
      a droplet of the ocean
      roll down
            from an eye

and you
who believes
      that mind answers

does not understand
yet
that mind answers
      only mind

and it

never able to
fully hear
nor answer
   silence

  or heart

  or destiny's
    breath

crossroad

for a moment
at any point
where infinite choices
narrow simply
        to four

and there
clarity
        calling
        yearning
        wanting
discovered when
looking far enough
down any choice
        we see the back
        of ourselves looking at
        the backside
        of ourselves
        looking back

        looking forward
and somewhere
in days
        behind
memory
that coloured light
speaks through
this rainbow mirror
        describing how
        it remembers
        sun and

i
here always
at these ever-present
forks in road
seeing neither
        front nor back
now shadow-less
        with light passing
        through

i, here
now

simply glass
becoming
        prismic heart

elders

you, who have
        come before
do not know
cannot hear
        your echoes glancing
        off tomorrow's light

the wearers
of today
        deaf to the breeze
beneath the cloak
        of yesterday's shadow
only watch
the daylight
        of motion

ever unsure

and unaware
of the warmth
        of whisper

wing

birds asleep

perched on charcoal grey branches
under roof's silhouetted eaves
        roosting at night

is it the light
        not the wind
beneath their wings
that would carry them
        as the sun rises and
        slowly floats into the sky

and the others

those birds whose destinies
command them to fly
through the black
        of the night

is it only their belief
in the light and
        searching between
or is it their raised wings
        unveiling their own
        tender light beneath

and either, each, all

beneath iridescent blue
or endless black sky
they, following their own trails

    calling wings back

in lines already drawn
        with the soft crayons
        of feather and down

time passage

this rocking
between
        being observer
        being observed
  between
        being present
        being gone

transcending
        dimension
        time

this place where
        i sit today
found its place
its shape
long before
my eyes could see

and i did not have
to be here in that
        time before
to see it now
        as it was then

transformed

i sit there now

the walls the same
wooden bar, the same
the wind,
the scent off
the lake, the same

the gulls, the maple
the poplar, the pine,
the same

the music of the breeze
        through the trees

a distant flute
notes reverberating
        echoing off the wind

candles, flames
        dancing slowly
the fire in the hearth
at the front of
this autumn night

and the conversations
flowing between those
peers, strangers, friends
their words somewhat
different there, then but
        the questions the same and

the door sits open
to remind the inside
of itself

to remind itself
of outside

and

reminding me

that i am
still
        here

red wind

riding the back
of the red wind today

effortlessly becoming
      my poetry

and not needing
nor wanting
to define

or to become
      the words

but becoming
instead
      the spaces between

those spaces
with infinite
invisible threads
between

between

and on a page
tying
one word
      to the other

within a life
tying
each
      to all

creation

i am not
this body
this place
this time
but
        all of this

i, here, but one
interconnected
infinitesimal
piece
of accumulated time

        from that first seed
        that first ember
        that first flash
        that first molecule
            of oxygen
        that first particle
            of sand
        that first droplet
            of water
        that first blade
            of grass

i
and each
of us
        alone

        together

the preface
        of hope

evening

at dusk
how many times
does the sky
wrap itself within
        veils of itself
until it dissolves
        into darkness

        and then

in that darkness
how many words
fall on top
of themselves
        in conversation
until they are lost
in themselves with
intersecting echoes
of unspoken word

bleeding then
        into silence

forest

again today
i walk
outside the path
through this
wood

in shaded
patterns
        a different
        path
patterns
        small pieces
        rays
        of colour
        light
flow, cut
through the trees and
        across my face

the birds
know me here
they do not fly
they accept me
        now
i, one with this
        a part of them

they no longer
        see me
they sense
        my scent
        and my colour
and trust
        the motion behind

there was a time
you and i walked
        this wood
        together
and you took my hand
in yours
and pointed
with the other
        to each new tree
        new bird
and told me
what they were called

and i knew
that even as you told me
        i would forget their names

we already
on the path
        from that language
and the words
given for them washed off
with the next
morning dew

                                        water ever
                                        washing
                                        that which
                                        is not part

and we walking

became another
        language

walking until
our words

all words

were lost
in the mist and
the intermittent
        falling rain

there
a silence coming
echoing its fullness
off the back
        of sky

mist falling through
washing language
and word
off lip
and ears

in the shadow
in the gentle rain
in the sunlight
        of silence

what is it that speaks
        here
            with such clarity

in this place
        without words

down

as we ride
the earth
      on the back
      of memory

memory as bird

bird with its
iridescent wings
      of hope
curled, folded legs
      of silence

everything nameless
each
all
on this global collage
of face

and everything each
again
with eyes

eyes looking within

and these
eyes tied to mind
      seeing always
      feather as chain

those tied to heart
      forever seeing
      both rock and wall
            as succulent down

echo

i know that
if i sit here
long enough
wearing
your words

that
in the distance
you would hear
their echo

and remember
where you had left them
search for them again

and in their finding
i would remember
why
         i wear them still

again

here in some
dark obscure
        place

in the middle
of an imaginary
        forest

in the middle
of an imaginary
        night

where no
        one goes

that no one knows

i am hiding

hiding
        from the light
        from the crowd
        from the noise
        from the voices

            within

but
they follow

they call out

like tiny brass
chimes
        in the middle
        of a cemetery

like a candle
in a cave
        in the distance
        in the dead of night

like copper bells
on the other side
        past cliffs that
        cannot be scaled
like tears in the eyes
of fate swelling
        looking down
        on animals grazing
        before the slaughtered flesh

like the tears that fall
remembering
        everything
        once

like the tears
already falling
from the trees
        giving themselves
        up to paper

        so that you

can read these
words
anywhere
        and

remember

your
dark obscure
        place

in the dead
of an imaginary
        night

in the middle of

name

i walk out
into the new light
of a new day

it pretending
that it does not
already know
        itself

pretending surprise
in seeing me here

it
already tied
by the heart
of all days
        past
tied
by the lucid
        multicoloured
        clairvoyant thread
of all days
yet coming

it whispers
        to memory
its soft fingers
already delicately touching
        the newer softer skin
        of destiny

and it is
it was
already here
	waiting for
	accepting
everything

already waiting
even for me
as i come
in my audacious breath
to give it
	a name

northern lights

on this edge
of a lone crow
screeching
at grey and white
      worrying clouds

a single leaf
tan brittle
hangs clinging still
to the smallest point
of an upper branch
      in a seemingly
         motionless afternoon

and

in a room painted
      in another colour
words are flying
off pages in a book

      words
      in another language

and they slide
out of empty windows

into whiffs of
a low smoke drifting
from an ancient limestone
      chimney nearby

that chimney today
carrying this new
smoke
  a scent unknown here

wood
  from another country

that wood
slowly falling
  shifting sliding
  beneath a moving flame
  dancing
wood
slipping
losing itself
  to ember

embers glowing
  golden
  then deep burgundy
  and lucid red

this colour
  turning
into white scent
  rising

rising
into sky

into this air of
        almost silence
this late autumn song
        before the snow

this echoed harmony
left hanging in the air

this song
this anthem
that a single leaf creates
        lilting against air's edge

        and then in its swaying
        final dance to the ground

there

here

silent music mixing
with smoke
riding
        forgotten words
        in another language
becoming
        low note on note
following invisible sheets
        of words lost
        a scent remembered
        and

i am but
ten days
        away

ten days
>	already coming

i had seen this day
>	since summer

and i told you
about it then

but

you did not listen

you did not believe

you were lost

in the language
>	of the green leaves

of the only trees
>	that grow here

and behind
the closed eyes
of the night
>	just falling

in passing

each moment
passing

stretching
expanding
      all those before
into memory
      and metaphor

each day that
comes
waits
      to fly
then nestles
      inside the palm
      of the one behind

each generation
the blood
flowing
contained
      of those before
      of those yet coming

each civilization
riding the shoulders
of that before
hanging onto the ankle
of that next one
      already anxious
      beginning to move

beyond, above
the universe
of other lifetimes
observes
   without eye
   without ear
   without lip
reaching through
that translucent colour
   of other, of self
reaching
through earth
through season
this blue and black sky

and with timeless
fingers
   pulls from
   the boxes of time

   unravelling the omniscient
   thread within and
sews
history to future
with the fine needle
of heart

shadows

on a knoll
of tall prairie grass
      still laden with dew
two shadows pass
      each carrying
      thought's echo

      yesterday's and
      tomorrow's sound

if we could but hear
if we could listen

its taste would caress
      our mouth
      our tongue
and gently flow
outward
in the breeze
      from our lips

but we
the conquerors
      have become

we
the creators
      without either true
      vision or speech

from the ancestors
      of rock and wheel
      of fire and cloth

from the ancestors
who rode this rock
  in circles
  around the sun
who rode through
  spinning circles
  of itself
  into day
  into night
through fire and ice
and wind
  carrying each

from the ancestors
who looked more
  without
  than within
pretending only
  to invent

with a stick
drew a circle
  in the sand
then stood it
  on its side
gave it a name
  calling it wheel

crushed the rock
to create stone
  to then build walls
and with flint
  sharpened arrow
  and spear
contained both
  fire and water

  as river wept

and now these
seeds
  of seed
  of seed
  of seed
fall from
trembling branches

these
  forgotten leaves

behind

behind the cloud
shadows
of earth

reflecting back
dulled image
      of sun
off mountain
flat plain
rock ledge
      over lake
waterfall
      cascading
stream
      slowly rolling
brook
      subtly hidden

and all
in the traces of eagle's
      flight over each
come now
your eyes
down
from the shade
      of that other life

remembering

calling back now
to the depth of things

remembering

the path of seed
is not the coming
       through soil
not even the growth
       of stem into blossom
but to blossom dropped
       back to seed again

remembering

the sour dullness
       in complacency

the jagged edges
of resentment
       that contentment
       carries within

remembering

that the edge
       of violet, burgundy
wears
       all sides of black

remembering

the fine threads
of that same colour
      tying eyes to heart

and this morning
at dawn
the sun red
      on the horizon
with four slivers
      of charcoal grey clouds
      cutting
      across its face and
the crescent moon
      higher but on
      this same side of sky and

i looked
into yesterday's mirror
and saw
      the next lifetime
      coming

lucid blue

lucid blue
on these edges
of grey

in these years
of the shorter
        nights
of the lower
        clouds
and the white hair
        coming

this new shade
of blue

the last

and i not knowing
        yet

its degree

or its depth

other side

you now
on the other
    side
of water
of shadows
    falling backward

of time
no longer believing
    in itself

of other
lifetimes remembering
    themselves

of others
still wishing
    to be

you who still
do not know
how many times
    i have watched a door open
    expecting to see
    your face come through
    and

the doors open

the doors close

to no one
to shadow
to whispers
    hanging
    within
    and

i
have never felt
    an emptiness
    like this

forests

beneath snow
covered trees
        lost in this forest

you whimper

you whisper

        as if no one
        can hear

but your voice
carried
        a hemisphere
        away

and there
your breath
fluttered
        a butterfly's wings

and for an instant
through its eyes
you saw
the next season
        waiting

as your fingers
slowly reached
for the railing
        of passage

        invisible
        gone

other

fiction
        and mirror

a leaf
falls
believing
        it is
        another colour

falls
believing
        the grass below
        knows its name
        and calls it out

falls
believing
        this breeze
        belongs to another
        season

and

it falls

through
a hole in
        this endless
        day

and into
a glass dream
        already
        broken

whispers

waiting

        for the whispers
        to come

the place
the eyes
        have already
        forgotten

these
whispers
        the air
        wears

tucked
just below
        on that other side
        of silence

        on this edge of
        intuition's
                sightless breath

whispers
        before language

whispers
        of pictures

whispers
moving
flying

carrying
      but the weight
      of shadow
           in the darkness

flying
through the holes
that time leaves
      when it
           forgets itself
      when
           the universe
           hesitates

in that corridor
      the dreams
           come through

before
      remembering

before
      knowing, even

before
      wanting

with eyes closed
      before
           thought
      before
           desire

this

this

this black
on black
on black
      on silence

before

      the whisper
           comes

renaissance

i.

a thousand years ago

and twelve hundred
        kilometres away
i
watched
        an ant crawl
        upon a shifting
        and sifting
                desert sand

i
under the shadow
        of a grey hawk

beneath black feathers
of hollow air
        holding glistening
        ebony eyes

ii.

here today

the lice
the termite
the roach

the maggot
the rat
the flea

       live in their own
            language
       in the only
       world
            that they know

they do not
know
that we have already
given them
       a name
       and a place

they do not
know
that they are not
       wanted
         yet
their worlds move
through
       instinctual eyes
       unglazed

their journeys flow
beyond contrivance
  of time
  of place

and they
each
  already knowing
  all that we don't

  knowing even all
  that we can
    never know

but
still from our
self-made pedestal
we forge
  with arrogant mind
  ungracious hand

we pave
  the earth
we fill
  the marsh
we raze
  the forests

as

the trees
left here stand
  only seemingly
  silent

    yet even their chlorophyll
            flowing within
            intuitively knows
that but for
        two atoms
                different
it too
        would be red

        and blood

distance

in the middle
of the motion

       there is a stillness

       watching

it is silence

it is the instant
       before birth

it is death
       in the distance

it is the air
       encircling

it is the past
       remembering
the future
       waiting

this

this

this stillness
       slightly stirring

it is alive

it is more
>than alive

it is eternal

it is more
>than eternal
more than
>a word

>yet

we do not
>see it

we

blinded
>by motion

we caught up
>in this surface
>of movement

lost

>to that rhythm
>>deeper
>to that effortless
>>dance
>to that endless
>>music flowing

>and

on the horizon

there

is a single breath

it is almost
        a sigh

it is almost
        inaudible

it is almost
        nothing

it is

        everything

Bruce Kauffman lives in Kingston, Ontario and is a poet, writer, editor and workshop facilitator. A chapbook of his poetry, *seed* (The Plowman), was published in 2005, a stand-alone poem, "streets" (Thee Hellbox Press) was published in 2009 and his first full collection of poetry, *The Texture of Days, in Ash and Leaf* (Hidden Brook Press), launched in January 2013. His latest two books, *a seed within* (an expansion of his original chapbook) and *The Silence Before the Whisper Come*s, both with Hidden Brook Press, will also launch in 2013.

His work has appeared in numerous periodicals and anthologies, including a book review in *The Antigonish Review* (fall /2010) for John Pigeau's *The Nothing Waltz* (Hidden Brook Press). His poetry has also appeared in two plays, *The Garbage and the Flowers* (2008) and *A Moveable Feast* (2009). His poem "destiny", appearing in his first collection, was shortlisted in the 1995 Poiesis Poetry Competition.

In 1997/1998 he was research editor and volunteer coordinator for a poetry short collection and reference manual, the Poiesis Poetry Guide (1998). In 2011 he coordinated and edited That Not Forgotten (Hidden Brook Press), a 400 page poetry/short fiction anthology of 118 locally tied poets and authors, launched in September 2012.

In May 2010, he began hosting a weekly spoken word radio show on CFRC 101.9fm (Queen's University, Kingston, ON) called "finding a voice" and now also hosts a blogspace for that show at: http://findingavoiceoncfrcfm.wordpress.com/. As well, he hosts a monthly open mic reading series called "poetry @ the artel" (launched in May, 2009), and now facilitates a quarterly series of "stream of consciousness" writing workshops in Kingston with plans to expand to outlying areas.

He is a member of a local writers group. He joined the Wintergreen Studios Press Advisory Board as Acquisitions and Poetry Editor in July, 2012 and in August, 2012 became the Canadian Editor of CCLA's *The Ambassador*. He is currently editing other work and working on his next poetry manuscript, and as well creating a 6 act, separately monologued play.

Contact: bruce.kauffman@hotmail.com

HBP books by Bruce Kauffman

(Order any of these books on Amazon or other e-stores around the world.)

The Texture of Days, in Ash and Leaf
— ISBN - 978-1-897475-86-7

a seed within
— ISBN - 978-1-897475-99-7

The Silence Before the Whisper Comes
— ISBN - 978-1-897475-89-0

That Not Forgotten - Anthology Editor
— ISBN - 978-1-897475-89-8

Cover Photographer Bio:

Eleanor Leonne Bennett is an internationally award winning photographer and visual artist. She is the CIWEM Young Environmental Photographer of The Year 2013 and has also won first place awards with National Geographic, The World Photography Organisation, Nature's Best Photography and The National Trust, to name but a few.

Eleanor's photography has been published in the *Telegraph*, *The Guardian*, *The British Journal of Psychiatry*, *Life Force Magazine*, *British Vogue* and as the cover of books and magazines extensively throughout the world. Her art is globally exhibited, having appeared in New York, Paris, London, Rome, Los Angeles, Hong Kong, Copenhagen, Washington, Canada, Spain, Japan and Australia amongst many other locations.

She was also the only person from the UK to have her work displayed in the National Geographic and the Airbus run "See The Bigger Picture" global exhibition tour with the United Nations International Year Of Biodiversity 2010. In 2012 her work received coverage on ABC Television.

Books in the North Shore Series
Find full information at
– http://www.HiddenBrookPress.com/b-NShore.html

2 Anthologies

Changing Ways is a book of prose by Cobourg area authors including: Jean Edgar Benitz, Patricia Calder, Fran O'Hara Campbell, Leonard D'Agostino, Shane Joseph, Brian Mullally. Editor: Jacob Hogeterp
 – Prose – ISBN – 978-1-897475-22-5

That Not Forgotten - Editor – Bruce Kauffman with 118 authors from the North Shore geographic area.
 – Prose and Poetry – ISBN – 978-1-897475-89-8

First set of five books

— M.E. Csamer – Kingston – *A Month Without Snow*
 – Prose – ISBN – 978-1-897475-87-2
— Elizabeth Greene – Kingston – *The Iron Shoes*
 – Poetry – ISBN – 978-1-897475-76-6
— Richard Grove – Brighton – *A Family Reunion*
 – Prose – ISBN – 978-1-897475-90-2
— R.D. Roy – Trenton – *A Pre emptive Kindness*
 – Prose – ISBN – 978-1-897475-80-3
— Eric Winter – Cobourg – *The Man In The Hat*
 – Poetry – ISBN – 978-1-897475-77-3

Second set of five books

— Janet Richards – Belleville – *Glass Skin*
 – Poetry – ISBN – 978-1-897475-01-0
— R.D. Roy – Trenton – *Three Cities*
 – Poetry – ISBN – 978-1-897475-96-4
— Wayne Schlepp – Cobourg – *The Darker Edges of the Sky*
 – Poetry – ISBN – 978-1-897475-99-5
— Benjamin Sheedy – Kingston – *A Centre in Which They Breed*
 – Poetry – ISBN – 978-1-897475-98-8
— Patricia Stone – Peterborough – *All Things Considered*
 – Prose – ISBN – 978-1-897475-04-1

Third set of five books

— Mark Clement – Cobourg – *Island In the Shadow*
  – Poetry – ISBN – 978-1-897475-08-9
— Anthony Donnelly – Brighton – *Fishbowl Fridays*
  – Prose – ISBN – 978-1-897475-02-7
— Chris Faiers – Marmora – *ZenRiver Poems & Haibun*
  – Poetry – ISBN – 978-1-897475-25-6
— Shane Joseph – Cobourg – *Fringe Dwellers* Second Edition
  – Prose – ISBN – 978-1-897475-44-7
— Deborah Panko – Cobourg – *Somewhat Elsewhere*
  – Poetry – ISBN – 978-1-897475-13-3

Forth set of five books

— Diane Dawber – Bath – *Driving, Braking and Getting out to Walk*
  – Poetry – ISBN – 978-1-897475-40-9
— Patrick Gray – Port Hope – *This Grace of Light*
  – Poetry – ISBN – 978-1-897475-34-8
— John Pigeau – Kingston – *The Nothing Waltz*
  – Prose – ISBN – 978-1-897475-37-9
— Mike Johnston – Cobourg – *Reflections Around the Sun*
  – Poetry – ISBN – 978-1-897475-38-6
— Kathryn MacDonald – Shannonville – *Calla & Édourd*
  – Prose – ISBN – 978-1-897475-39-3

Fifth set of three books

— Tara Kainer – Kingston – *When I Think On Your Lives*
  – Poetry– ISBN – 978-1-897475-68-3
— Morgan Wade – Kingston – *The Last Stoic*
  – Novel – ISBN – 978-1-897475-63-8
— Kathryn MacDonald – Shannonville – *A Breeze You Whisper*
  – Poetry – ISBN – 978-1-897475-66-9

Sixth set of three books

— Bruce Kauffman – Kingston – *The Texture of Days, in Ash and Leaf*
   – Poetry – ISBN - 978-1-897475-86-7
— Chris Faiers – Marmora – *Eel Pie Island Dharma: A hippie memoir/haibun*
   – A memoir in haibun form – ISBN - 978-1-897475-92-8
— Theodore Michael Christou – Kingston – *an overbearing eye*
   – Poety – ISBN – 978-1-897475-93-5

Seventh set of four books

— Alyssa Cooper – Kingston – *Cold Breath of Life*
   – Poetry – ISBN – 978-1-927725-02-3
— Bruce Kauffman – Kingston – *The Silence Before the Whisper Comes*
   – Poetry – ISBN – 978-1-897475-98-0
— Sarah Richardson – Kingston – *Before I Lose Light*
   – Poetry – ISBN – 978-1-927725-05-4
— G. W. Rasberry – Kingston – *More Naked Than Ever*
   – Poetry – ISBN – 978-1-927725-04-7

www.ingramcontent.com/pod-product-compliance
Lightning Source LLC
Chambersburg PA
CBHW031125080526
44587CB00011B/1118